An Old Timer's Logic

Geriatric Grey Matter...That Matters

Ray W. Maher

Copyright © 2025 by Ray W. Maher

All rights reserved. No part of this publication may be reproduced, distributed, or transmitted in any form by any means, including photocopying, recording, or other electronic methods without the prior written permission of the author, except in the case of brief quotations embodied in reviews and certain other noncommercial uses permitted by copyright law. For permission requests, write to the author.

Cover Design by Ray Maher
Edited by Carolin Petersen of Tigerpetal Press
Typeset in Arno Pro and Aptos
First Edition 2025

ISBN 978-1-0690700-6-7   (paperback)
ISBN 978-1-0690700-7-4   (ebook)

Scripture taken from the HOLY BIBLE, NEW INTERNATIONAL VERSION. Copyright c 1973, 1978, 1984, International Bible Society. Used by permission of Zondervan Bible Publishers.

www.raymondmaher.com

Table of Contents

Free Verse Poetry Explained	1
Poems & Prose	3
POETRY SECTION ONE	
Harvesting Leaves	8
Me Not You	9
My Nature Walks in the City Core	10
Walking Hand and Hand	12
Fading Kinship and Affiliation	14
Be Prepared for the Unexpected	15
No Regrets – Dead and Gone	16
My Staple of Life	17
Mistakes That Haunt	18
My Absolute Serenity	19
Not too Old to Hear My Inner Child	20
Red: The Color of Learning	22
My Three-Part Fall Fair	23
Haunted by Something Small	24
Camping in Cemeteries	25
Little Billy Bob	26
Not Exactly a Holiday	28
I am God's Clay	30
Body and Soul	32
Power of Pain	32
Elders Like Me	33
The Artist	33
A Time of My Prose	34
Contagious Problems	35
An Example of My Life, Written at 64	37

Another Example of My Life, Written at 80	40
The Faith of Older Christians	43
Takes One to Know One	47
Crossing the Finish Line	50

POETRY SECTION TWO

Saskatchewan	54
Big Business Prairie Style	56
Fickle, Familiar, Fatal	57
A Perfect Day	58
The Empty Pew	59
Married	60
Places of Remembrance	61
Once	62
One Door In – One Door Out	64
Christmas Eve	66
My Christmas Wish	66
The Fraser	67
Just Call Me Mean	68
Friendship Freely Given	72
Enslaved in 2023	74
References	75
Acknowledgements	77
About the Poet	78

Free Verse Poetry Explained

So, you ask, "What in thunder is Free Verse Poetry?"
Free verse is any form of poetry that does not rely on consistent patterns of rhyme and meter. In fact, free-verse poetry doesn't have to rhyme at all.

As a result, free verse tends to follow the rhythm of natural speech.

However, a natural rhythm may still emerge despite the lack of a specific metrical structure.

Poets still also use alliteration, rhythms and other poetic techniques to create their desired effect. They may also use rhyme, but it's usually irregular.

A word from your Old Timer poet
The elderly are often viewed skeptically when it comes to their wisdom and insights. Don't dismiss us as old geezers, codgers, coots, or fossils in life. Even if someone is one hundred, they *may still* have clear-sightedness about what is important in life.

No specific age guarantees discernment or wisdom, but I hope you will take on the modern view about age. The view that 80 is the new threshold for "old," with many people still active and engaged in life between 80 and 100+.

We old timers are people of longevity who strive for:
POSITIVITY: Despite facing the probability of health concerns with each passing year, many of us view our remaining years as our time for new beginnings, learning, and continued contribution rather than just a period of decline. I believe old age isn't just about a

number but also about an individual's physical and mental capabilities, social engagement, and sense of purpose.

As we grow older, we may need to move to collective dwellings: places where we can receive care and support such as seniors' residences or nursing care facilities. Some remain independent, living in their own home or apartments. Don't resent or fear us, just hear us with respect, for you may become old too before you realize it.

I hope you enjoy *An Old Timer's Logic*.

Sincerely,
Ray W. Maher *an old timer*

Part A: Poems and Prose

We are the people of longevity.
No overtime, fixed income.
Work pensions never go up.
Expenses never come down.

It is reported that 69% of people seventy-five and older own their own home,[1] meaning that their wealth sits in their homes and retirement savings. That does not mean they are on Easy Street. Their homes are the result of years of paying a mortgage. In my experience, home ownership for them was no easier in their day than it is today.

There are financial realities that temper their home equity. Between the ages of 75 and 100, many will develop one to four chronic illnesses, such as high blood pressure, diabetes, etc., meaning they must subsume the ongoing cost of prescriptions.[3] Many will need to sell their homes and move into a senior residence or nursing home for more in depth care.

One of the greatest fears of people of longevity is that they will outlive their money.[1] The life expectancy in Canada is 82 years,[2] but the number of people living in their eighties and nineties keeps growing. Recent Statistics Canada data shows that the country's population of people over 100 years has more than tripled between the years 2000 and 2023, from 3,393 up to 11,705.[2] That makes centenarians the fastest growing age group in Canada, and the agency says their numbers are poised to rise almost ten times higher over the next half-century.

We are people of Longevity
Dentures common, so's own teeth,
Take them out to clean or brush in mouth.
Dentures must fit snug! Cavities still blight!

While many seniors retain their natural teeth, edentulism (toothlessness) is more prevalent in this age group, potentially affecting their overall health.[4]

Dental insurance coverage varies among seniors, with a lower proportion of older Canadians having their dental expenses covered by insurance compared to younger adults.[4]

Around 60% of seniors visited a dental professional in the past year, while a substantial 21% avoided visits due to cost, according to Statistique Canada.[3]

We are people of longevity.
We suffer chronic pain, long-lasting, persistent,
and reoccurring.
It impacts our quality of life,
not like the pain of daily news, cannot be turned off.

Approximately one in three seniors (33%) living in private households experience chronic pain. This number is higher (38%) for those in long-term care institutions.[5]

Osteoarthritis and rheumatoid arthritis are major contributors to chronic pain in older adults.[3]

Diabetic neuropathy, a type of nerve damage, is a significant cause of chronic pain in seniors.[3]

Cancer itself or its treatments can lead to chronic pain.[3]

INJURIES AND PAST MEDICAL EVENTS: Surgery: Post-surgical pain can become chronic if not properly managed.

PAST INJURIES: Old injuries, even if seemingly healed, can contribute to long-term pain.[5]

We are people of longevity.
The target of scammers. Crooks out to hurt,
trick and deceive us.
They make their lies, believable truths.
We are sheep among wolves – dedicated to fleecing us.

Seniors are disproportionately targeted by scammers, with significant financial losses reported annually. One in ten seniors are targeted by scams every year.[6]

Seniors may be less likely to question suspicious requests.

They may lack familiarity with technology, and online scams can make seniors more susceptible.

Seniors living alone or lacking close family support may be more vulnerable to scams.

Scammers use increasingly sophisticated methods, including AI to clone voices and create fake websites, making it harder to detect fraudulent activity.

We are people of longevity.
Some of us are silver foxes, some skin-headed bald.
Old boy hair everything in between the two.
No matter, if hairless, can be loved and love.

In Canada, approximately 53% of men and 37% of women aged 65 and older experience some degree of baldness or hair thinning.[7]

Hair loss becomes more prevalent with age, with the highest percentages of baldness occurring in the 75–100 age group.

We are people of longevity.
Our adult children, see us as their kids to be tended to.
Tell us what to do for our own good and safety,
Will we bless them for this or not?
Is it pay back time for them, or pay up time for us?

Older parents who may require more support and caregiving from their adult children because of health issues may lead to more demands, dependency, and a reversal of roles.

Role change can cause stress/strain as aging parents grapple with a loss of control and adult children take on more caregiving responsibilities while also juggling their own family and personal lives.

Poetry Section One:

Please note that each person of longevity is unique and everyone has their own food for thought, to share with you.

These free verses are my thoughts for you to chew on.

Harvesting Leaves

I rake abundant leaves,
laying as discarded litter,
covering the ground.

Do I blame the trees,
for the vast yield?

Or the winds who blow
leaves everywhere?
Leaving them anywhere,
they please!

No blame! For trees or winds.
For life,
like leaves,
yields beyond our control.

And life is best
when I take what I find,
randomly assigned me,
and in my mind,
receive it, as if,
it suits me,
perfectly fine!

Me Not You

FEELING stopped,
ignored, dismissed, dropped!
My dreams crack and crumble under me.

FEELING put in my place, by my reality.
Bludgeoned hopes slap my face,
leaving me battered, with empty illusions.

FEELING sorry for myself,
Sour at others, critical, as one without power.
Stuck, standing solidly in self-centeredness.

FEELING I WANT TO BE THE SUN! WITH:

Everyone and everything
Revolving around me!
So, my dreams can come true – just for me,
because selfishness is bad for you!

My Nature Walks in the City Core

Oh, for a home beside
a woodland glade
where my visits
would not cease or fade.

But I live in
the city's downtown core.
Where nature is
held to the very least.
Except for the trees
gentrifying the beast.

On my daily walks,
I greet the trees,
who grow and
flourish in the traffic's smog.
Faithfully lining streets
crowded with plodding
indifferent sods.

Late evenings
sometimes I find,
My trees alone
in silence kind,
For traffic is gone,
and their peace is sublime.

In my city's downtown core,
trees are sentinels
of life and peace.
Reminders to show us
nature's grace,
in the city's cement face.

Walking Hand in Hand

You can see the old couple walking most days.
She has a cane to balance her tilted sways.
Secure with his hand in hers, and her cane in the other.

Balanced, they go around the block.
On days she's feeling extra strong, they go to the clock,
It's at Five Corners, in the heart of historic downtown.

He is stout and short, and she matches him, but less so, stout.
What was he once? Was she a mother? It doesn't matter!
There are lots of old ones about, as visible as the homeless.

He wears a red jacket, and she still wears her covid mask.
They don't litter, disturb, yell, swear, or add graffiti as they pass,
They share the sidewalk, do not text or talk on phones as they walk.

Walking, they survey houses and yards on neighboring streets.
Enjoying the architecture and curb appeal, rejoicing in some,
Wondering why others are so unloved, unkempt, and neglected.

Their world has shrunk to their condo, and two cats.
Yes, they have children and grandchildren, but not nearby.
Yet they're heart close, as distance makes love grow stronger.

They are content with a few church friends. He curls; she knits.
Busy with Doctor's appointments, lab tests, and prescriptions
They're thankful despite cataracts and chronic pain.

Both accept the age card dealt to them. There's no reshuffle.
They encourage each other to play their age card with patience,
Waiting in peace for God to play His face card as He's ready.

David's Logic   Ecclesiastes 8:7,8
"Since no man knows the future, who can tell him what is to come?
No man has power over the wind to contain it; so no one has
power over the day of his death."

Fading Kinship and Affiliation

This old timer agrees
that our society is getting worse.
For the gracious spirit of brotherhood,
Languishes!
Growing fainter in its power,
than a single word uttered
in the coal mine's depth.

Likewise, fraternity is ignored,
lost in a raucous babble,
of self-proclaimed experts,
defaming and blaming each other.

Confusion reigns,
in the autocratic use of power,
not my brother's keeper, **me**, and **mine** only count
justified in the name of power and money.

Be Prepared for the Unexpected

It's good to be prepared, ready with plans,
Especially, ample provisions,
for possible emergencies.
But don't forget,
solid plans, can unravel.

Our present world is fixated -
on being one-step ahead.
Yet the one most difficult to control,
may be oneself.
Do we want to rule fate itself,
as if, we are gods?

Preparations may open the door,
to success, or not!
All our fussing, planning, concocting,
and devising,
may be for nothing,
because of unforeseen actions.

Each day has an independent streak.
Unplanned circumstances and events,
may disrupt your schedule,
by having things go their way,
not the way you planned.

No Regrets – Dead and Gone

In nature, autumn leaves are dead witnesses,
to their termination.
Their lives cut short.
By the trees, they nourished and nurtured.

They were callously eliminated,
as if they never existed.
In a dispassionate seasonal adjustment!
Simply sentenced to permanent layoff.
As those no longer wanted or needed.

Too many folks live like trees,
Cancelling others from their lives.
Dropping them dead, as no longer needed.
They declutter their life at will.
Practicing legal assassination
Rendering another dead while alive
With not even a ghost of remembrance.

My Staple of Life

Apples may date back to the Garden of Eden,
the Bible says that Eve ate forbidden fruit
not necessarily an apple.
perhaps a fig would suit.

If it was an apple, did the serpent whisper?
"Apples are so heavenly to eat, but so much more,
as apple pie, sauce, strudel,
or as cider galore!"

Apples still make me pause and think of choice,
Will I snack on them or use them for much more,
Easy apple sauce or demanding pie or strudel?

Did a doctor really say?
"An apple a day keeps the doctor away?"
It doesn't matter to me
As I raise my hand in a salute to them,
As apples are so much more,
As wonderous desserts at home or in the store.

Apples are healthiest plain, not in desserts.
Apple desserts expand the waistline.

Mistakes That Haunt

Some mistakes are of little consequence,
others come back to torment us and others.

It seems we repeat mistakes, when we get away
without paying an immediate price or penalty.

How many times can we drink and drive without problems?
How many times can we gamble, with our lives and the lives of others?

We are free to do self-destructive things, that endanger us, and others.
Our choices have the power of good or evil for us and our victims.

It's not just alcohol and drugs that have the power to destroy us,
but anything, even food can enslave us in addiction.

My Absolute Serenity

In this present world of endless layers of complexity,
where wrong is argued right, because,
absolute right is every person's opinion,
so, fact and fiction get blurred,
beyond any true recognition.
I find my sanctuary in a true black or white space.

It's my lawn and garden,
my place of clarity about right or wrong.

A weed is a weed,
and the grass needs cutting or not.
The simplicity of the tomatoes, ready to pick or too green.
No one advocating or opposing any cause or issue.
The welcome silence of grass, earth, and sun before me.

In my yard I am the master of undisputed right or wrong,
because I garden alone.
Being your own boss means you get the fame,
and the blame.

Not too Old to Hear My Inner Child

It's late fall as the cat and I watch
flying leaves raining outside the window.

An icy wind twists the tree branches
swooping up their last leaves and flying them about,
like swarming birds, diving high and low,
far and wide.

It is a tussle between the pull of winter
and the slipping grip of fall.

The advance of winter looms before me,
and awakens my inner child.
Ready and alert to the promise of winter,
excited to the delights of ice skating, snowball fights,
and so much more.

My inner child that loved to jump in piles of leaves,
to play in the rain,
wade through snow drifts,
layered up and scoffed at the cold,
pokes me!
He asks, why it's no longer so with me?

And I answer that
I'm no longer a child,
full of life like the wind.
Now I'm old and content,
to keep an easy-does-it grip,
on life, as long as I can.

David's Logic   Ecclesiastes 9:4
"Anyone who is among the living has hope - even a live dog is better off than a dead lion!"

Red: The Color of Learning

Red means blood flowing from a cut,
or the fire of learning burning in my gut.

Long ago, I attended a one-room country school
where a giant Maple tree adorned itself each fall in red.

I do not know if the yellow brick school still stands,
called S.S. #6 Warwick, Public School, grades 1 to 8, no kindergarten.

We who filled the desks have long ago moved on. Also…
the solo teacher, our books, blackboards, and woodstove heat.

School was my blood transfusion of life, beyond our farm.
Which was,
a world of chores, barn, garden, hens, pigs, cows, and brother rows.

In first grade, we began with fat pencils, making straight lines and circles,
before printing, my lines were crooked and my circles messy
do-overs.

Grade one was rocky for me, but I passed from grade to grade,
Enjoying most subjects, and one teacher inspired to be one too.

I can never attend that one-room country school again, but it
left me red hot in the need of learning, for as long as I live.
There is so much to learn at every age especially at mine.

My Three-Part Fall Fair

Our fair was a three-in-one delight.
Parade, Exhibits, and Midway bright.

Watch, wave, and applaud at the parade.
explore and linger at favourite displays and demonstrations.

On the midway,
lose your stomach on rides – or feed it.

Every year the fair impressed with
the promise of some new attraction.

Always the old favourites, so hard to resist,
Candy floss, or fried onions on a hot dog?

Some preferred, striking with bumper cars
Or the scrambler to dizzy their brain.

Some got stuck at the top of a Ferris wheel,
And learned to pray, to touch the ground again.

As a child the fair was magical.
Magical as an old timer can mean,
grandchildren having conversations with me,
rather than others on their cell phones.

Haunted By Something Small

Something small once had the power to haunt me,
I believed there was a living vampire in my room.

As a young child, I awoke in my bed,
to the sound of a bat flying over my head.

I covered my head with my sheet, but I was still terrorized,
by the sound of wings zooming around my bed.

I shivered under the covers, cowering and certain that,
the bat could get caught in my hair and would need to be cut out of it.

I had heard from other kids, that bats can drink your blood,
or bite you and give you rabies, a terrible death.

When would others wake up to the sound of the bat?
I was certain I would suffocate under the covers before my rescue!

Since I'm telling this story – I didn't die!
A little brown bat did not drink my blood or bite me
or get caught in my hair.

But my brothers teased me for fearing a little bat.

But fear can make small things enormous when your little,
and sometimes this still happens when you're an adult too.

Camping In Cemeteries

My mom didn't have much money,
But she was always bright and sunny.
When we were on our trip west,
Looking for someplace to nest.

We traveled in an old camper van,
Bought privately from junk yard, Dan.
Just us three, my mom, brother John, and me.

Mom always said that we'd know where,
We were going when we got there.
We didn't know her heart was set on B.C.
Three provinces away.

Because money was tight
We found that cemeteries on the outskirts of places,
Were gracious to us with welcome spaces, to camp.

We would arrive at dark, and stay the night,
And leave in the morning's light.

Many foolish folks are squeamish about graveyards,
To us, as campers, needing a place to rest, they were the best.
No one ever bothered us there.

As an old timer now, I'm not squeamish,
about the graveyard that awaits me.
I am just glad I don't know the date,
when my ashes are scheduled to arrive there.

Little Billy Bob

Grade one made Billy Bob tired.
He wanted to stay home, in bed, instead.

His teacher always wanted more and more,
Endless lessons and activities were a chore.

Then there was a Halloween Party in his class,
His costume was tight, and his face mask, smothering!
What a silly fuss causing him needless suffering.

His parents loved to take him trick or treating,
He thought they walked too far, with no retreating,
Before it was finally done.

Billy Bob wondered,
Why not just give him some candy and chips at home,
And be done with it.

Billy Bob found it embarrassing, yelling, "Trick or Treat!"
At strangers' doors he wasn't supposed to talk to,
Adults made everything complicated.

One very cranky man asked him,
"What trick will you play on me, kid?"
"None," Billy Bob stuttered, "I don't even want to be here!"
"I understand, lad, neither do I," the man said,
Giving him extra candy.

How many children are doing things,
that their parents are more excited about than they are?

Solomon's Logic   Proverbs 20:11
"Even a child is known by his actions, by whether his conduct is pure and right."

Not Exactly a Holiday

When I was a boy, many years ago,
Thanksgiving Day wasn't a holiday at our place.

The whole family from the oldest to the youngest,
Celebrated the day by harvesting our farm garden.

Our deep, dark, damp cellar was ready for the produce.
Dad and my two oldest brothers dug the potato hills,
Spilling out potatoes, on the ground, for me,
To rub off their dirt, and place them in drying piles,
After a couple of hours, they went into burlap sacks,
To be stacked after a wagon ride to the basement.

Mother and my sisters dug the carrots and cut off their tops,
Sending them by the wheelbarrow to the cellar's wooden box.
Next, they cut cabbage heads, hard and round,

Lastly, they gathered cooking onions in mesh storage bags,
To hang on nails on the cellar's big wooden beam above my head.

We all picked off popcorn cobs from their stocks, shucking their coats,
Making them fit to be stored and hung on hooks in the back kitchen.

We harvested a few small pumpkins that shared a cellar table,
With many Hubbard and acorn squash, the last produce of our harvest.

On a farm, holidays seldom meant no work.

Working on a holiday today can mean extra pay for every hour worked.
We never thought of getting any pay when we worked as a family, on Thanksgiving Day.

I am God's Clay

Just as I am
From dust to dust
As common as dirt
As low as the earth
As fickle as blowing soil
As unyielding as the ground.

Nothing to commend me
Nothing to offer but the little I am
A little bit of worthless clay
In need of a good potter.

For the potter
Takes a little clay
Shapes it
Into that which becomes
A work of Art.

The potter deals
With his clay
As he sees best
And shapes it to his
Purpose and pleasure
To accomplish his glory.

Lord, please
make me as your clay.

Turn me in Your hand
anyway, You care to.

Shape and mould me
as Your work of art,
to Your glory.

Body and Soul

Sick
Seek
Doctor
For Medicine
For Your Body.

Also Seek God
For Peace
For Your Soul

Power of Pain

Pain
isn't seen –
but felt.

Yet it,
makes us see,
how good –
life felt,
without it.

Elders Like Me

See down from the sky,
From five storeys high.

Which means
we live in bird houses,
called condos,
with clean windows!

The Artist

Sees
All Nature
All People
All Animals
His to Paint Alive

To become as dead on his canvas.

A Time of My Prose

Wise Ways? To Greet a New Day

   ***ONE:** Crawl, not spring, out of bed. Slowly stand up.
   Act confused about whether you're awake, in a bad dream, or about to be struck by lightning.
   Realize you need the bathroom and stagger to it.
   When you reach it, the danger of lightning is past.
   NO! It's no time to look in the mirror.
   TWO: Spring out of bed like a streak of lightning, sing in the shower, be cheerful, and drive the sane ones in your family mad.
   THREE: Approach your day like a mountain climber about to summit your profession.
   You will be at the peak if you remember where you put your keys.
   FOUR: Approach your day as a burnt-out light bulb, knowing you could be replaced at anytime.
   Be defiant; face your years until retirement with a pain in your neck and a whine on your tongue.
   FIVE: Set your alarm one hour before you need to get up, let it buzz and beep, and don't get out of bed for one hour.
   Teach your alarm that you will not get up until you want to do so!
   SIX: We longevity folks are full of jokes, about waking up on any given morning.
   Because we're relieved and glad every day it happens.

*Number One is the way I greet the day as an Old Timer

Contagious Problems

Life hands us trouble in four sizes, small, medium, large, and oversized.

Each size tips and spills from others to us – and we tip and spill trouble on others.

Influencing Others
Max Bryce is a veterinarian whose life is cracking apart like thin ice under his feet. He is suffering from festering desperation. No longer in control of his emotions, his simmering stress is now boiling like a dangerous thunderstorm on the horizon. No one suspects that their town's veterinarian could expose them to the hazards of his personal problems.

Many innocent folks in Max's town and rural community of York Mills will have his dilemma spill on them. *Reflection from suspense thriller Trapped at Birth.*

Some peoples' desperation makes for a good thriller novel because people want to know what happens to a person who becomes stretched to his or her breaking point. Some things stretch people of longevity to the snapping point.

What do you know about the real and often unrecognized difficulties among people of longevity? Let me share with you:

Statistics on Senior Loneliness and Isolation:
PREVALENCE OF LONELINESS: Almost one in five Canadian seniors (65+) report experiencing loneliness, according to Statistics Canada.[8]

GENDER DIFFERENCES: Senior women are more likely to report feeling lonely than men.[8]

MARITAL STATUS: Seniors who are widowed, separated, or divorced are significantly more likely to be lonely than those who are married or in common-law relationships.[8]

INCOME LEVEL: Seniors with lower incomes are more likely to report loneliness.[8]

AGE: Older seniors (85+) are more likely to report loneliness than younger seniors (65-74).[8]

SOCIAL BARRIERS: Nearly one in four seniors experience barriers to social participation, which is strongly linked to loneliness.[8]

HEALTH IMPACTS: Loneliness is linked to increased risks of dementia, heart disease, stroke, depression, and anxiety. It can also lead to a higher risk of premature death.[8]

As people slide along in life from 75 to 100, they may not go out but need people to come to them. Visits of family and friends can shatter the loneliness and isolation that people of longevity experience.

An Example of My Life, Written at 64

Printed in an anthology published by Polar Expressions

Thriving or Surviving in Retirement

At sixty-three years young I graduated from a real job to 'Retirement.' So here I am, living the celebrated dream of countless workers. Is retirement a blissful dream come true or is it a nightmare? Am I one of the happy pensioners? Am I thriving or surviving? I'm hesitant to say. After almost a year of retirement, perhaps I should be an expert on the subject, but I'm not. I have learned a few things about retirement, however.

I find complaining doesn't help in retirement. In retirement you no longer need to deal with your job and coworkers, but you still have to put up with yourself – *no small task for some of us!* At work, there was always someone who would gladly complain and whine with you. In retirement, you whine alone.

I'm finding that my mate has no sympathy for my complaining. In retirement, my advice is to never complain to your spouse about anything. They will take it as an invitation to share their complaints about you. Being home means there seems to be a lot of things you do and don't do that are not appreciated by your mate.

Remember the honeymoon period after marriage, when learning to live together was a big deal? It was such a big deal you both quit trying. You endured dealing with a mate who was hard to change. Then, you settled into live and let live. Next, you stuck together as Mom and Dad because your children were out to get both of you.

In retirement, your children are grown and gone – at least sometimes. Many of us retire to a tiny house to discourage forty-year-old children from living in the guest room or recreation room. You also learn the art of saying you are short of money and wonder if they, your grown children, could spare you any this month. This is not because you need it but if you don't ask them first, they will be asking you.

Boundaries can become blurred in retirement. Before we retired, my mate and I went to our jobs and did not interfere with each other's work. It was to be similar in retirement. The inside was to be her domain. The outside of the house was to be mine. I garden and cut the lawn, she doesn't. She was to have the kitchen she wanted. She cooks; I try not to. We have been married forty years, but we may need another forty years to hold us steady.

The inside-outside thing turned out to be a silly theory. Of course, I had to have my say about living room paint color that caused vomiting in the day and nightmares in the night. My wife forbade dusty miller and geraniums in a front flower garden. She insisted I plant pattypan squash in the vegetable garden – *no one really eats pattypan squash; it's a seed-company lie, but she would not listen.* This inside-outside boundary thing is not resolving itself in retirement.

Most of retirement is a balance between the extremes of thriving or hardly surviving. Personally, I have little patience for senior braggers who claim they are thriving endlessly. Their lavish tales exaggerate summer days full of golfing, fishing, tennis, biking, hiking, camping, with endless barbeques or garden parties. In the winter they are snoozing and cruising in exotic, sunny, warm spots like the Caribbean Sea.

For myself, I do the chores of the seasons. I cut the lawn or shovel snow. I paint the gazebo or force myself to go to the gym. My travel is to the grocery and hardware stores. I feed the birds and pet the cats. I get less done with more time to do it as I lose and forget things along the way.

I see this retirement thing as a lifestyle where thriving and just surviving are permanently blurred into one mixture of both. Retirement is neither the best of times nor the worst of times. It's the same as the rest of life: a hash of thriving and surviving.

Retirement Waltz Poem
Written in the first year of my retirement.

The fulltime quickstep of a job has ended.
No half-time or quarter time work either!
So, the unemployed dance goes on and on
A dance that has no required time signature
To tell me where I am – or should be.

The retirement waltz
Has me dancing out of step –
No longer leading, but following -
Left to bounce around like a shadow
Of my working life of forty years.

The band plays on
With no patience for me.
I know those who can't dance
Need to get off the dance floor.
But the retirement waltz
Holds me tight!
It will not let me sit the damn dance out!

Another Example of My Life, Written at 80

Published July 2025 in The Chilliwack Progress

Both Half Empty and Half Full

Today, I put my wife's cancer quilt over her as she shivered in her hospital bed. She made that quilt after her first bout with Cancer twenty years ago. I read the quilt, which testifies in capital letters that **CANCER CANNOT DO ELEVEN THINGS**.

It cannot destroy peace, erode confidence, erase memories, stifle laughter, corrode faith, kill friendship, invade the soul, steal humour, conquer the spirit, silence courage, or shatter hope.

Such a positive list encourages those cornered and caught by Cancer, but as one who is walking beside my wife in her third attempt to escape from the stranglehold of Cancer, the list is both true and false.

In February of this year, when we learned my wife was diagnosed with three spots of liver cancer, our peace was shattered. Our confidence was also eroded.

Marilyn, my courageous warrior wife, struggled free of ovarian Cancer in her first bout in the ring with Cancer.

Next, she escaped colon cancer, but its wound remains in the missing part of her large intestine.

Now, she faces liver cancer. Indeed, this present reality has shaken our confidence in facing one more battle with Cancer. How many times can a person get up and keep fighting?

For those who have been untouched by Cancer, it is the silent killer hiding itself inside one's body while gaining an advantage in attacking its victim on the sly.

It also murders the memory of a life untouched by Cancer. As every cancer survivor lives with the realization, their Cancer may return even after a significant number of years of being cancer-free.

So yes, Cancer can invade one's soul, threaten one's spirit, and corrode one's faith. It is a total invasion of both body and soul.

Cancer is more sinister than just attacking cells and body parts and functions. It invades the mind with fear, shattering one's courage and hope.

Yes, Cancer can stifle laughter, steal humor, and limit friendships. It will do all of these to some degree at certain times during a person's war with Cancer.

Seeing a glass half full shows a positive attitude. But seeing the glass half empty is an honest response to reality.

Calling the glass half full or half empty is the exact measure of the water in the glass.

The list of eleven things Cancer cannot do means sometimes they are true for those fighting Cancer, and sometimes they are not.

There is a common point of view that those held in the grip of Cancer should display a positive attitude of confidence, courage, and hope. This attitude is said to be about what's best for the person with Cancer. It is really about what feels most comfortable for family, friends, and medical personnel.

The most common question we ask of another is – How are you? We hope for a positive response, but we may not expect or want to hear the truth about how they feel. Remember, it is not about encouraging others to tell you what you want to hear from them.

Allow and encourage cancer patients to share how they feel, their pain, discomfort, discouragement, concerns, and doubts.

If you were getting assaulted by Cancer, wouldn't you want to vent your feelings freely, the negative ones as well as any positive ones?

Life for cancer patients is one day at a time. Treatments and their side effects are unique to each patient. Yet all patients endure the soul-wrenching waiting for their treatment results, knowing they may be good or bad news.

In some ways, it seems one's battle with Cancer is faced alone. But then there is the realization that countless others are fighting for their lives against Cancer, too.

No one wants to be part of cancer statistics, such as 2 in 5 Canadians are expected to be diagnosed with Cancer in their lifetime. Approximately 1 in 4 Canadians are expected to die of the disease.

I asked my wife if she agreed that the Cancer Cannot Do statements on her quilt were both true and false. She said when she made the quilt, she did not see them as statements of truth but as slogans to inspire cancer patients battling Cancer and those who are cancer survivors.

She also said when you are facing Cancer, it seems to hold all the power, but the Cancer Cannot slogans are declarations of resistance in one's battle with Cancer. She felt other cancer patients might repeat some or all of them like a mantra as a way of meditating or mind control against Cancer's assaults.

My wife's hope isn't in slogans but in God, for death comes to all, with or without Cancer. She trusts Him as more powerful and gracious than Cancer or death. She looks forward to being in the presence of God in the new heaven and new earth.

Her hope is found in Revelation 21:1-4. He will dwell with them, and they shall be his people, and God himself will be with them; [4] he will wipe away every tear from their eyes, and death shall be no more, neither shall there be mourning nor crying nor pain anymore, for the former things have passed away.

The Faith of Older Christians

Older Seniors find their faith often seems out of step with children and grandchildren. They experience the generational shift that has occurred with younger generations. Increasing numbers of younger generations identify as having no religious affiliation.

Many older Canadians (65+) still identify as Christian. Christianity remains more prevalent in certain provinces, like Newfoundland, where over 82% of the population identifies as Christian.[9]

While Christianity is dominant, other religions like Islam, Hinduism, Sikhism, and Buddhism have seen growth in Canada.[9]

What's the Use of Wondering?

A Story of Grace that is Undeserved Love from a Christian Perspective.
ME: Hi, how are you?
(I'm thinking that: *You may vaguely recognize me but you cannot remember my name or how you know me. You look at me carefully, hoping my name will come to you soon.*)
YOU: Hi, how are you?
ME: I'm good, and my work is going well.
YOU: Where do you work now?
ME: The same place as before. By the way, I talked to your mom on Sunday, and she is doing well despite her divorce. She said that you have been a great support to her.
YOU: I am surprised she talked to you about that. Did she tell you that her whole forty-year marriage was a merry-go-round of deceit and unfaithfulness by her husband, my dad? My mother believed

they had an ideal marriage and that Dad was innocent of any affairs outside their marriage until Dad served her with divorce papers.

ME: Innocent people often have no sense that those they love are guilty of betrayal towards them. I understand your father never missed a chance to tell your mother he loved her. Your mom says that he acted devotedly to her and you. She admits that she never considered that her husband, Stan, could be unfaithful and love another woman while married to her. Common sense can cause one to wonder about a marriage partner, but pure love for a spouse can be much stronger than common sense.

YOU: My mom's love was blind concerning dad. She still considers him her husband even though they're divorced, and he's run away with another woman. She's sad but says there was no use in wondering about him when he was her husband. It would have been a life of suspicions and spying for her, and it wouldn't have stopped his affairs. She gave him the benefit of her love and trust. He abused them. There is no trust for her now, but she is sticking with her love for him. She's keeping her vow to love him as long as she lives. She will not stop loving him just because he no longer loves her.

ME: I agree with your mother. I am pleased she is honouring her marriage vow made before God. It is much better to keep loving others even if they hurt and desert us.

YOU: Well, that is the stupidest thing I've heard in a long time. My dad, her husband, is a cheating jerk who does not deserve my mom's or my love. He abandoned us. He is selfish and untrustworthy. Who are you anyway? How do you know my mom?

ME: I'm your parents' pastor, Pastor Mike, from St. Paul's Church. I recognize you from worshipping with your parents at Christmas, Easter, and other occasions during the year.

YOU: I didn't recognize you without your robes. I have only seen you at church. Meeting you here in your regular clothes at the shopping mall made you look a little familiar, but nothing more. Going to church weekly didn't do my father much good. Did it, Pastor Mike?

ME: Your dad didn't come to services weekly, about half the time or less. Your mom is there every Sunday. Going to church cannot guarantee people will be faithful spouses. But it can encourage those who are willing to love God and to love others steadfastly. Sin is a reality of life. Being unfaithful to a spouse is sinful, but one of many sins. You may be guilty of sins.

YOU: Even if I sin, my sins do not make my father any less of a cheating jerk. They do not undo his affairs or a broken marriage. The truth that we all sin only proves that going to church is a waste of time, Pastor Mike.

ME: Many people would agree with you.

YOU: Is that all you can say? Where is your defense of the church and God? You pastors act as if you and God have things under control when everything is out of control, a carousel of emptiness covered in lies.

ME: Like yourself, people are often frustrated with me because I cannot assure them that God will give us lives that are spared the hurt of sin that someone else committed. Sin is real. It results sooner or later in hurt and brokenness or worse. When people are hurting, it is easy to blame those whom they see as the sinner, the one who hurt them through their sins. God will help those wounded by another person's sin. God will help anyone who will give Him their hurts and sins.

YOU: God, if he really exists, should prevent sin from happening in the first place. However, I must be excused, Pastor, as I have an appointment soon.

ME: Certainly, I do not wish to make you late, but I believe you have answered why churches are not worthless. In them, God encourages people not to sin in the first place, so they spare themselves and others from the pain and brokenness of sin.

YOU: Maybe, you're right, Pastor Mike, but I don't think so. Thanks for supporting my mom. Bye.

ME: I'm pleased to do so. Good-bye.

It Takes One to Know One

*People of longevity find new words used to describe what we referred to with a different name.

In the last several years a certain political leader on the world stage has been described by the word "narcissist". This led me to research the word. In the past a narcissist was called a *know-it-all meaning someone who cannot be reasoned with*. Below is a story I wrote about my research.

Are there more narcissists presently than in the past? Has there been a mass production of entitled, self-centred, arrogant individuals with inflated opinions of their importance? Am I the only one to think there are more egotists than ever?

Why do I get so irritated by folk who think the world revolves around them? You may be thinking that it takes one to know one. Could I be a narcissist myself? I don't think I am. Yet, it's hard for me to know myself objectively.

Friedrich Nietzsche has observed that our own self is well hidden from us. Carl Jung suggests that everything that irritates us about others can lead us to an understanding of ourselves. I am not convinced Jung is correct, but here I am exploring what annoys me about narcissists to see if it can result in a better understanding of myself.

I researched what is labeled as a narcissistic personality disorder according to the Mayo Clinic, the National Institute of Health, and other sources. Many people have narcissistic traits, but in some individuals, their view of themselves is so distorted that they have an unreasonably high sense of their own importance. It is tiresome and dangerous to deal with them personally when they are in positions of authority or political power. My study is limited and centered on what irritates me about narcissists and what I can learn from my annoyance.

Why do I reject someone with a grandiose sense of self-importance? It's a gut-level rejection. Self-esteem has its limits. To feel the world revolves around me or you is a lie in my thinking. Even if a person is seen as very capable and talented in their job, they are never so good that they can't be replaced with someone considered better than them. Sometimes, unless I do something, it won't be done, right? No one in my family argues that I clean the cat litter box best. Being the best or claiming to be the best is not a cause for boasting. Being the best is a very temporary achievement.

It is said narcissists cannot accept the word, 'no,' and are insulted to be called, 'average.' A narcissistic personality feels superior to others and wants to be recognized as such. They think they are entitled to the best, the most, and the nicest life has to offer.

I do not deserve the best job, the most money, or the nicest things. Yet, I have thought I am entitled to a good job, affordable housing, a livable wage, good health, and a long life instead of being thankful for having any of those things.

Solomon, of Biblical fame, observed that our lives are more than we think we deserve or are entitled to. He cautions us to remember, "The race is not to the swift or the battle to the strong, nor does food come to the wise or wealth to the brilliant, or favour to the learned; but time and chance happen to them all." (Ecclesiastes 9:11 NIV)

Everyone wants to be accepted, respected, and seen as valuable. Yet, even at our best, we will be challenged and criticized. It is observed that narcissistic folk have trouble handling anything that seems like criticism and become impatient or angry when challenged. Egocentric people may belittle others who have differing opinions. They are unable to understand anything but their point of view. It is always someone else at fault or to be blamed. Their self-esteem, which appears limitless, is too fragile to accept any slight, real or perceived.

Labeling others is easy and commonplace. If we put a label on someone, we will treat them according to the tag we assigned them. I do not treat everyone the same way. We tend to treat people the way we see them. I will treat friends, family members, and work associates positively. People I don't know, I may approach cautiously. I admit that there are some individuals whom I ignore. We may directly or indirectly abuse or harm others in many ways because we have assigned them a particular brand.

My study of narcissistic behaviour has proven Carl Jung correct in that what irritates me about narcissists is seeing myself in them. They hold up a mirror to me – a mirror I would rather ignore than face honestly. Jung's point is that I cannot change narcissistic individuals who irritate me, but I can do something about my actions that reflect their characteristics.

It's not about others who are carried away with themselves. It is about my own tendencies to see myself as superior to others, believing that I know best and that others are wrong, and my need to control and act as if I am God. After my study of narcissistic behaviour, I still do not believe I am a narcissist. Still, I have some serious narcissistic characteristics that I need to deal with instead of being irritated at others who remind me of myself.

Crossing the Finish Line

Written when I was 77 years old.

A possible motto for people of longevity might be "We aren't what we used to be – but love us as we are!"

Ideally, when the finish line for a race is imminent, all the runners are spurred on to be the first to cross it. However, crossing the finish line is not in my best interest at seventy-seven. The finish line of life is no longer a small dot on the horizon.

My age group is trying to slow down on the track of life with all our remaining fibres. For us, the finish line ahead belongs to the Grim Reaper. We are not cowards, just not in any rush to cross the extermination line that could trip us up at any time.

I have gone over many finish lines related to my natural development. I have gone past being an adorable baby, the youngest of six children. My childhood on a farm and attending a one-room country school with grades one through eight are long gone. Yes, high school and college are long over.

Yes, there is so much in the past and much not finished for me. Still, I am involved in various roles as a husband, father, grandfather, lead on a curling team, a good cook, and a gardener. Still trying to master my lack of patience, my wish-I-hadn't outbursts of temper, and my bad habit of blaming and judging others instead of only myself.

Do any of us ever cross the finish line of becoming full-fledged, totally mature, and responsible adults who live supremely happily as long as we live? In theory, crossing a finish line is simple. You start at the starting line, and at the signal, you run around the track towards the finish line. But I believe the race of life is about encouraging other racers as we run our own race. Life isn't about competition but running so everyone wins.

Life is both how others count and when they are discounted. Retired seniors like me are seen as being past our best-before date. Retirement is a finish line at which your job or profession ends. For some of us, it is hard to adjust to a life without employment. Some thrive without work, doing what they please. But most know they are on a dead-end stretch of life.

The bodies and minds of seniors show signs of wearing out and needing repairs and patches. Our sharpness and vitality vary from day to day. All of us old ones are unique, and we differ in our energy, physical health, and mental well-being.

We oldies face the most variety of finish and starting lines as a group. Our lives become blurred between what was and what is no longer. Commonly, eyesight diminishes with cataracts, and hearing goes from *clear* to hearing very *little*. And our ability to lift *most* things becomes limited to *some* things. And our remembering ranges from every detail to it *may come to me later*. And our walking can go from *OK* to walking with a *cane*, or *walker*, and then *a motorized cart*. We must get on waiting lists for knee and hip replacements.

Don't pity us. Let us do that ourselves. Don't shun us or ignore us as if we would waste your time, especially if you are related to one of us. Instead, consider taking our motto to heart. Our motto is, "We aren't what we used to be – but love us as we are now."

I must disagree with some seniors who want to threaten their indifferent family members. They want it remembered that older people have power. Their power is their capacity to change their will toward those ignoring them.

Threats do not work. Being old does not mean our families will or must love us. Genuine love is a gift given to others freely without guilt or pressure. As I see it, "Treat us as those worthy of your love, and we will do the same to you." You, too, will be old one day, and the finish line of life will no longer be a dot on the horizon but getting clearer and larger daily.

David's Logic   Ecclesiastes 5:15
"Naked a man comes from his mother's womb, and as he comes, so he departs. He takes nothing from his labor that he can carry in his hand."

Poetry Section Two

Saskatchewan

Published in Poetry Elite, A 1985 Anthology of Canadian Poetry

A land that cannot be owned,
Like an independent cat, it owns you.
One only endures the extremes of climate,
And delights in its beauty,
Its vast farms, sprinkled population,
And grain elevators.
Do not begin to dominate
The strength and might of nature.

Nothing in Saskatchewan is moderated,
Everything stands stark and sharp.
Summer days of bright endless sun and heat.
Limitless winter days of frigid, crackling cold.
Nights of blinding pitch – blackness
Or brilliant bright moonlightedness.
Days of expanding, endless sky, or closed days of grey.

A people rich in many cultures and heritages,
Fiercely Canadian, yet uniquely
Independent and self-determined.
Truly of Prairie nature and yet
Distinctive of western sisters.
Strong in N.D.P.'s and Conservatives
But lacking Liberals.
Loyal to native-born,
Rich in family ties.

Suspicious of Ottawa
And reluctant to accept
Those not her own.
Yet with a generous nature,
Willing to help others in need.
Those of Saskatchewan reflect
The dominance of nature, independence and strength.

Big Business Prairie Style

*Written about twenty years after poem "Saskatchewan" in 1985.
In this later poem, grain elevators in every town were disappearing
from the landscape.*

Big farms and less people
Big grain and cattle country
Gone are the small family mixed farms
Of the pioneer yesterdays.

Specialization
Crops air seeded
Over stubble.

Farms the size of empires
Machinery too big for –
The road…

School buses,
New pickup trucks,
Skidoos,
Independence reigns.

A neighbour-less prairie
Only a few home
On the range
Today!

Fickle, Familiar, Fatal

Published May 2007 Good Times Magazine Poetry

Frigid, fierce, long white winters,
Fickle, reluctant, warm spring days,
Fleeting, frying-hot summers.
Fatal, early frosts…
Familiar seasons that
Form us as
Saskatchewan
Prairie people.

A Perfect Day

Published April 2009 Good Times Magazine Poetry

        A day of solitude
             No one home
                  But me
            And the cat
    Who has gone
        Back to bed
Under the quilt cover.

        No hurry needed,
    Nothing I have to do
          That cannot wait.

        Open to endless
    Personal possibilities,
Or just doing nothing at all
            If I should see fit.

        For it is a perfect day
           To be still and sit
                Really no need
            To start or to quit.

The Empty Pew

The faithful numbers grow smaller
Younger ones disappear into themselves like turtles,
Indifferent to God, and the faith of parents.
Each secure –
In the heaven and hell
Of their own making.

Married

But not for better
But for the worse!
Love and marriage
Do not go together like a
Horse and carriage –
More like the togetherness
Of lions and hyenas!

Our love has turned sour and rancid.
Now, it's not love but hate!
We're both saying:
"Let me count the endless ways –
That everything is your fault,
And everyone knows it's true, but you –
Even after, all that I have done
To change what's wrong with you."

Places of Remembrance

Nov. 11, every year
we remember Flanders Fields with crosses, row on row,
so far away from the cenotaph near us.
It stands ignored as we pass it any other day of the year.
Only on Nov. 11, do we stop, watch, and pray.

Our cenotaph's very presence in our midst,
demands nothing from us,
but begs us to remember,
those who lost their lives,
in wars before now.

Many ignore our past and refuse its place,
in shaping our present state of grace –
our freedom today from yesterday's tyranny.

Remembrance calls us to take up the torch of honour and appreciation,
for those who died, fighting for our freedom costing their lives.

As of 2023, Veteran's Affairs database listed over 9,000 military memorials across Canada which includes cenotaphs.

Once

Once when I was younger, twenty to be exact,
I knew more than,
my parents
and many others.

For being young
assured me,
when it came to them
I was simply wiser.

Once I was married,
and had my own children –
in humility, I learned,
I was not wiser than,
my parents!

I was not making a better job,
of raising my children than they had done.
We think everything should be simple –
until we do it.

Once I had grandchildren,
they helped me find,
the truth!

It's not about being wiser or better,
but love is the best, test in living –
it makes us and others equal –
not better or worse!

Solomon's Logic   Proverbs 23:22
"Listen to your father, who gave you life, and do not despise your mother when she is old."

One Door In – One Door Out

Each of us is a door
To ourselves
Where we
Come in
And
Go Out
In our thoughts and actions.

Sometimes we come into ourselves
And lock the door.
We need our private sanctuary
Time to mend
Our hearts, minds, and souls.
We crave peace and rest.

Sometimes we go out of ourselves.
To meet others
For companionship, fellowship,
And community.

In our lives we have
A private locked door of self.
And a public open door
Where we mingle and mix with others.

Our Challenge is one of balance,
Private or Public Door
Each door is a gift for our life,
Too much of either –
Means Loner or Party Animal!

David's Logic   Ecclesiastes 7:18
"Avoid all extremes."

Christmas Eve

On Christmas Eve,
even the most resistant,
may be found, in Church.

Celebrating Christ's Birth,
that shows God's love and peace,
for all the earth.

My Christmas Wish

No longer bubbling with excitement for Christmas presents
like children anticipating gifts they have hoped for.

Yet, I yearn for gifts that cannot be bought,
gifts that must be offered, not sought,
but given in love by others.

Oh, for big loving hugs of grandkids,
Unexpected visits from old friends,
Caring phone calls from family far away
People gifts – not things.

The Fraser

*A river in British Columbia Canada that was searched for gold.
Published in* The Deadly Five *a historical fiction novel, in 2020*

Dirty brown river hurrying along,
filled with mean pride and spirit.
Treacherous water but –
tempting with placer gold.

Homegrown, back in distant mountain peaks,
a razor cutting rock and pushing land.
Bending and stretching in long winding flow
to empty in the ocean far below.

Scorning us foolish folk – here,
to poke and choke out your gold.
You have laid the snare to get rich,
ready to watch us die trying.

Just Call Me Mean

His siblings called him,
Mean, instead of Mike.
And mean, he was too,
as he bossed them left and right.

But it was the way
His father raised him.
A giant-sized blacksmith of a dad
who worked the boy
like he was a man – not a lad.

He wanted Mike his oldest to become
tough, strong, and if he was mean –
it wasn't bad.

It was important to his dad, that,
his boy should know how to fight with might,
if others didn't treat him right

The boy didn't need encouragement
To clobber, wallop, batter, wrestle and grapple
Until he won each fight.

He grew into the brute size of his dad
And was afraid of almost none.
He was his father's son, a success story.

But fate has a way of undoing upbringings
by people we do not know –
in this story, one by the name of Nate.

Nate never learned the art of fighting
because he was a slip of a young man
who lacked great size and strength
but was afraid of almost none
because he knew how to
run, climb, duck, dive, dance, and hide.

Nate happen to walk in the street by the blacksmith shop,
when Mike was standing at its open door.
"You lost, Bean Pole?" he called sneeringly.
"Maybe so," Nate answered good naturedly, stopping in the street.

"I like to fight so make yourself scarce, Bean Pole."

"You look too big and heavy for fighting, to me."

"Come over here and I'll slap you silly! You skinny runt."

"Waddle over here and I'll race you down the street and back to here."

"If I come to you, I'll break your legs, and you won't be running."

A crowd had gathered to see and hear
the blacksmith's son and the stranger.
One in the crowd said to Nate,
"Best move along he's as mean as his old man."

"Thanks for the advice; they're probably not mean,
just misguided," Nate replied.
The man roared with laughter and shouted,
"He just said the blacksmith and his son
aren't mean, just misguided."
The whole crowd joined in laughing.

The blacksmith had joined his son at the shop's open door.
He stepped from his door and yelled,
"I dare anyone of you to tell me to my face,
I'm mean or misguided!"
The crowd became silent, fast.

The blacksmith proud of himself, added to the silence,
"You're all a bunch of cowards.
Get out of my sight, starting with the trouble-making
stranger in the street."

"I beg your pardon sir, but,
I challenged your son to come and race me,
down the street and back to here.
He didn't come out to race me because he is afraid he may not win."

"He's not afraid, but he's a fighter not a runner," the blacksmith
snarled.

"I believe that's true, that's why I'll race him down the street.
I'm a racer not a fighter.
Doesn't that make sense to you?"

"It makes sense to do what you need to do. So what of it?" answered the blacksmith.

"The point is that your son doesn't need to fight me or others.
Is your son fighting it to avoid harm to himself,
or to prove he's strong and can beat up others?
Shouldn't he know that he can do that by now?"

"He needs to show how strong he is so people will fear him."
"Fear doesn't lead to respect but resentment and dislike."

"Whether people like him or not doesn't matter," the father insisted.

"It may not to you, but it will to him.
It's misguided to go through life without being respected,
as fear has a limited power over others," Nate said.

Then everyone jumped because no sooner than the words left Nate's mouth,
and the thunder rolled, and the lightning flashed,
and the rain poured on them
and they all raced for cover.

The moral of the poem is simple; don't be mean and try to get respect by beating up other people.

Friendship Freely Given

This poem was published in Harvest a Collection of New Canadian Poetry 2012. *It was in a slightly different form there.*

When I first met Joe…
His scorching intensity was like the sun, on the hottest summer day.
His handshake was crushingly forceful on my arthritic hand, nearly causing tears.

He was all a top executive needs to be,
confident, competitive, clearly tall, fit and firm in body and mind.
The possibility of him extending me genuine friendship,
seemed remote.

When I first met Jude…
He was bright sunshine,
warm and inviting, neither hot nor burning.

His handshake was warm, courteous –
relaxed not bruising.

He was an ordinary fellow, self-secure, like well-worn shoes.
The chance of a friendship with him,
seemed almost certain.

When I first met Jason…
He was the mystery of a person of a different race.
There was no handshake in his culture.

Instead, a ready smile and eagerness to know and be known.
Both confident and vulnerable in his interaction.
He offered me friendship as if, it had always been there between us.

Solomon's Logic   Proverbs 18:1
"An unfriendly man pursues selfish ends."

Proverbs 17:17
"A friend loves at all times and a brother is born for adversity."

Enslaved in 2023

Baffling world!
Enslaved people in our time and place,
captive by their handheld devices, before their faces
unaware of where they're walking in their distracted paces.

Indentured to the frenzied furor of a public craze.
Held in social media's roaring and consuming blaze.
Constant rovers, pirating their time in a daze of waste.

Dominated as slaves, living in tech power, subjection,
consumed and addicted to their vice,
for egocentric hours and hours.

References

1. Charlebois, Brieanna. "Meet the Centenarians: Canada's Oldest Age Group Is Also Its Fastest-Growing | CBC News." CBCnews, June 26, 2024. https://www.cbc.ca/news/canada/british-columbia/canada-centenarians-fastest-growing-1.7246790.
2. Canada,. 2024. "The Daily — Key Findings from the Health of Canadians Report, 2024." Statcan.gc.ca. 2024. https://www150.statcan.gc.ca/n1/daily-quotidien/250305/dq250305a-eng.htm.
3. Canada, Public Health Agency of. 2021. "Aging and Chronic Diseases: A Profile of Canadian Seniors." Www.canada.ca. July 14, 2021. https://www.canada.ca/en/public-health/services/publications/diseases-conditions/aging-chronic-diseases-profile-canadian-seniors-report.html#a3.
4. Carrly McDiarmid. 2019. "This Is a Health Fact Sheet about Oral Care Habits, Visits to Dental Professionals, Dental Insurance, and Cost Barriers for the Canadian Population Aged 12 and Older. The Results Shown Are Based on Data from the Canadian Community Health Survey." Statcan.gc.ca. Government of Canada, Statistics Canada. September 16, 2019. https://www150.statcan.gc.ca/n1/pub/82-625-x/2019001/article/00010-eng.htm.
5. Health Canada. 2021. "Canadian Pain Task Force Report: March 2021." Www.canada.ca. May 5, 2021. https://www.canada.ca/en/health-canada/corporate/about-health-canada/public-engagement/external-advisory-bodies/canadian-pain-task-force/report-2021.html.

6 and, Employment. 2024. "What Every Older Canadian Should Know About: Fraud and Scams - Canada.ca." Canada.ca. 2024. https://www.canada.ca/en/employment-social-development/corporate/seniors-forum-federal-provincial-territorial/fraud-scams.html.

7 Ocampo-Garza, SoniaSofía, Alessia Villani, Maria Ferrillo, Gabriella Fabbrocini, Massimiliano Scalvenzi, and Angelo Ruggiero. 2022. "Hair Aging and Hair Disorders in Elderly Patients." International Journal of Trichology 14 (6): 191. https://doi.org/10.4103/ijt.ijt_90_21.

8 Government of Canada, Statistics Canada. 2023. "A Look at Loneliness among Seniors." Www.statcan.gc.ca. November 3, 2023. https://www.statcan.gc.ca/o1/en/plus/4881-look-loneliness-among-seniors.

9 Statistics Canada. 2021. "Religion in Canada." Www150.Statcan.gc.ca. October 28, 2021. https://www150.statcan.gc.ca/n1/pub/11-627-m/11-627-m2021079-eng.htm.

Acknowledgements

"An Example of My Life, Written at 64"
   Printed in an anthology published by *Polar Expressions*

"Another Example of My Life, Written at 80"
   Published July 2025 in *The Chilliwack Progress*

"Saskatchewan"
   Published in *Poetry Elite, A 1985 Anthology of Canadian Poetry*

"Fickle, Familiar, Fatal"
   Published May 2007 *Good Times Magazine Poetry*

"A Perfect Day"
   Published April 2009 *Good Times Magazine Poetry*

"The Fraser"
   Published in *The Deadly Five,* a historical fiction novel, in 2020

"Friendship Freely Given"
   Published in *Harvest a Collection of New Canadian Poetry 2012.*

Author/Poet Ray W. Maher

Before retirement, Maher was defined by his professions as a schoolteacher and an ordained clergy person. In retirement, he writes, gardens, curls, and cycles on his bike. He lives with his wife of fifty-eight years, Marilyn, in Chilliwack, British Columbia.

Thus far, he has penned three novels. His first two, *The Deadly Five* and *The Second Five,* are historical fiction novels set during the Fraser River Gold Rush of 1858. His third book, *Trapped at Birth With Only One Way Out,* is a mystery, thriller, suspense story of a man on the run.

He has been writing poetry since his boyhood, and his love of poetry was deepened in high school, where memorizing it was a required activity. One of his early poems as a boy was put to music. Free Verse poetry of Ogden Nash and others inspired his preference for his style of poetry.

Reader's Poems/Notes

Reader's Poems/Notes

www.ingramcontent.com/pod-product-compliance
Lightning Source LLC
Chambersburg PA
CBHW060341080526
44584CB00013B/863